Sentimientos

Vergüenza

Sarah Medina

Ilustrado por Jo Brooker

Heinemann Library
Chicago, Illinois

© 2008 Heinemann Library
a division of Reed Elsevier Inc.
Chicago, Illinois

Customer Service 888–454–2279
Visit our website at www.heinemannlibrary.com

Photo research by Erica Martin
Designed by Jo Malivoire
Color Reproduction by Dot Gradations Ltd, UK
Translation into Spanish produced by DoubleO Publishing Services
Printed in China by South China Printing Company Limited

12 11 10 09 08
10 9 8 7 6 5 4 3 2 1

ISBN 13: 978-1-4329-0630-6 (hb)   978-1-4329-0638-2 (pb)
ISBN 10: 1-4329-0630-5 (hb)   1-4329-0638-0 (pb)

Library of Congress Cataloging-in-Publication Data
Medina, Sarah, 1960-
  [Embarrassed. Spanish]
  Vergüenza / Sarah Medina ; Ilustrado por Jo Brooker.
      p. cm. -- (Sentimientos)
  ISBN-13: 978-1-4329-0630-6 (hb)
  ISBN-13: 978-1-4329-0638-2 (pb)
  1. Embarrassment--Juvenile literature. I. Brooker, Jo, 1957- II. Title.
  BF575.E53M4313 2008
  152.4--dc22
                              2007038612

Acknowledgments
The author and publisher are grateful to the following for permission to reproduce copyright material: Bananastock p. **22A, B, C**; Istrock/Slobo p. **22D**.

Every effort has been made to contact copyright holders of any material reproduced in this book. Any omissions will be rectified in subsequent printings if notice is given to the publisher.

Contenido

Algunas palabras aparecen en negrita, **como éstas**. Están explicadas en el glosario de la página 23.

¿Qué es la vergüenza?

La vergüenza es un **sentimiento**. Los sentimientos son algo que sientes en tu interior. Todos tenemos diferentes sentimientos todo el tiempo.

tristeza

felicidad

celos

Cuando te sientes avergonzado, te sientes **incómodo** delante de otras personas.

¿Qué ocurre cuando me siento avergonzado?

Cuando estás avergonzado, es posible que sientas calor y las mejillas se te pongan rojas. Incluso te pueden dar ganas de llorar.

Puede ser difícil hablarles a las personas.
Puedes tener miedo de decir una tontería.

7

¿Por qué me siento avergonzado?

Puedes sentirte avergonzado si muchas personas te miran.

Puedes sentirte avergonzado si alguien
se ríe de ti.

9

¿Está bien sentirse avergonzado?

Todos nos sentimos avergonzados alguna vez.
La vergüenza es normal.

Si te sientes avergonzado, algunas personas te entenderán e intentarán hacerte sentir mejor.

¿Qué puedo hacer si me siento avergonzado?

Si te sientes avergonzado, díselo a personas que se interesen por ti. Te ayudarán.

La vergüenza puede hacer que quieras esconderte. Recuerda que las cosas no son tan malas como piensas.

¿Me sentiré avergonzado siempre?

Es normal que los **sentimientos** cambien.
No siempre te sentirás avergonzado.

14

Cuando te avergüenzas, te sientes mal pero no por mucho tiempo.

¿Cómo sé si alguien se siente avergonzado?

Cuando algunas personas están avergonzadas, puede que no quieran hablar. Puede que quieran estar solas.

Puede que se cubran la cara o que no puedan permanecer quietos.

¿Puedo ayudar a alguien que se sienta avergonzado?

Puedes ayudar a las personas cuando están avergonzadas. Sé amable y nunca te **burles** de ellas.

Hazles saber que te caen bien y que quieres ser su amigo.

¿Soy el único que se siente avergonzado?

Recuerda que todos nos sentimos avergonzados algunas veces. La vergüenza es un **sentimiento** normal.

Es bueno saber lo que puedes hacer cuando te sientes avergonzado. Así puedes ayudarte a ti mismo y ayudar a otras personas.

¿Qué son estos sentimientos?

A

B

C

D

¿Cuál de estos niños parece avergonzado?

¿Qué sienten los otros niños?

Mira la página 24 para ver las respuestas.

Glosario ilustrado

burlarse

decir algo desagradable,
como broma o para ofender
a alguien

incómodo

no sentirse a gusto

sentimiento

algo que sientes en tu
interior. La vergüenza es
un sentimiento.

Índice

Respuestas a las preguntas de la página 22

El niño en la foto D parece estar avergonzado.
Los otros niños podrían sentirse enojados, orgullosos
o bondadosos.

Nota a padres y maestros

Leer para informarse es parte importante del desarrollo de la lectura
en el niño. El aprendizaje comienza con una pregunta sobre algo.
Ayuden a los niños a imaginar que son investigadores y anímenlos
a hacer preguntas sobre el mundo que los rodea. Muchos capítulos
en este libro comienzan con una pregunta. Lean juntos la pregunta.
Fíjensen en las imágenes. Hablen sobre cuál piensan que puede ser
la respuesta. Después, lean el texto para averiguar si sus predicciones
fueron correctas. Piensen en otras preguntas que podrían hacer sobre
el tema y comenten dónde podrían encontrar las respuestas. Ayuden
a los niños a utilizar el glosario ilustrado y el índice para practicar
vocabulario nuevo y destrezas de investigación.

For William, Robin, Fiona
& Danielle. It takes a village.

Published in 2021 by Groundwood Books / House of Anansi Press
groundwoodbooks.com

Groundwood Books respectfully acknowledges that the land on which we operate is the Traditional Territory of many Nations, including the Anishinabeg, the Wendat and the Haudenosaunee. It is also the Treaty Lands of the Mississaugas of the Credit.

We gratefully acknowledge for their financial support of our publishing program the Canada Council for the Arts, the Ontario Arts Council and the Government of Canada.

Library and Archives Canada Cataloguing in Publication
Title: The house next door / Claudine Crangle.
Names: Crangle, Claudine, author, illustrator.
Identifiers: Canadiana (print) 20200390368 | Canadiana (ebook) 20200390430 | ISBN 9781773063683 (hardcover) | ISBN 9781773063690 (EPUB) | ISBN 9781773063706 (Kindle)
Classification: LCC PS8605.R36 H68 2021 | DDC jC813/.6—dc23

The illustrations in this book are a combination of paper construction and various printmaking techniques.
Design by Michael Solomon
Printed and bound in South Korea

Canada Council for the Arts   Conseil des Arts du Canada

ONTARIO ARTS COUNCIL
CONSEIL DES ARTS DE L'ONTARIO
an Ontario government agency
un organisme du gouvernement de l'Ontario

With the participation of the Government of Canada
Avec la participation du gouvernement du Canada | Canada

MIX
Paper from responsible sources
www.fsc.org   FSC® C013572

THE HOUSE NEXT DOOR

CLAUDINE CRANGLE

GROUNDWOOD BOOKS
HOUSE OF ANANSI PRESS
TORONTO / BERKELEY

ALL alone, in an open field stood a house.

A sturdy little house, built a long time ago, from trees that once grew right where he stood.

Through his front windows, he watched over long grasses that waved in the wind.

The grasses could bend in the wind, but the little house had to stand his ground.

Sometimes the wind blew with such force that it whistled and howled right through his walls.

In the spring, driving rainstorms rattled his shutters.

And in the winter, great snowdrifts would pile up against his back wall.

The harshest winds came from behind,
so his back shutters were closed.

This was his lot.

Season after season the sturdy little house held his own.

Until the day the wind blew something unexpected his way.

A new house had arrived.

No — two houses.

One was off in the distance to the right.

The other was off to the left, quite far away.

Through his side windows he could see them.

Slowly, he pulled his side shutters closed.

Then he bolted them tight.

Just like the back windows.

And so the years passed.

With back and side windows shuttered,
the little house watched over his field.

He weathered the seasons and held firm
against the wind.

Until one spring day, which began in the most unusual way.

His floors rumbled and shook.

His walls trembled.

He looked out the front windows.

A long gash had torn right
through the middle of his field.

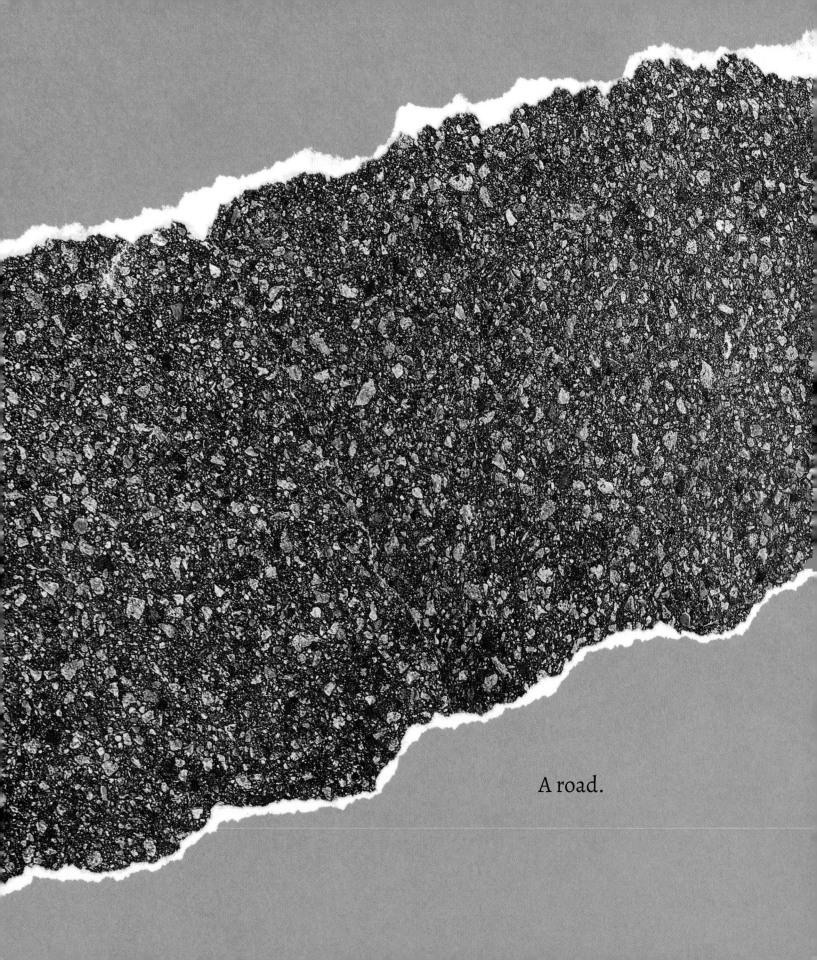

A road.

Soon they began moving in.

They lined up along the road.

And the road began branching into more roads.

And more of them arrived.

Row upon row of blank faces stared back at the little house.

He slammed his front
shutters shut.

And waited in the dark.

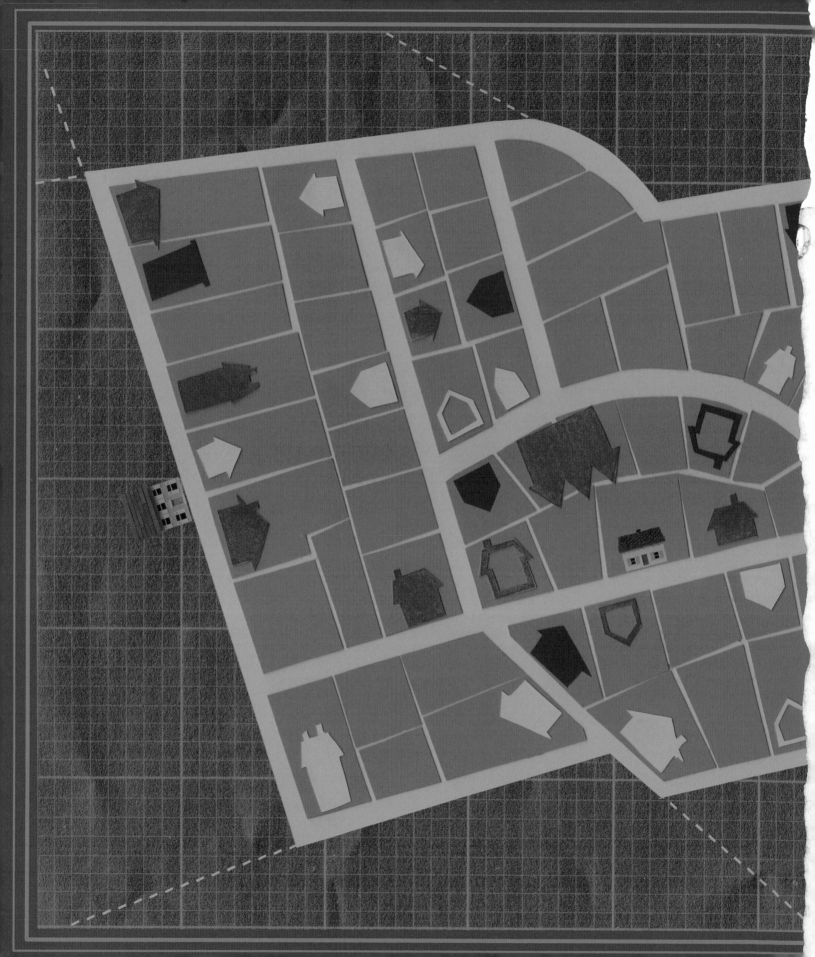

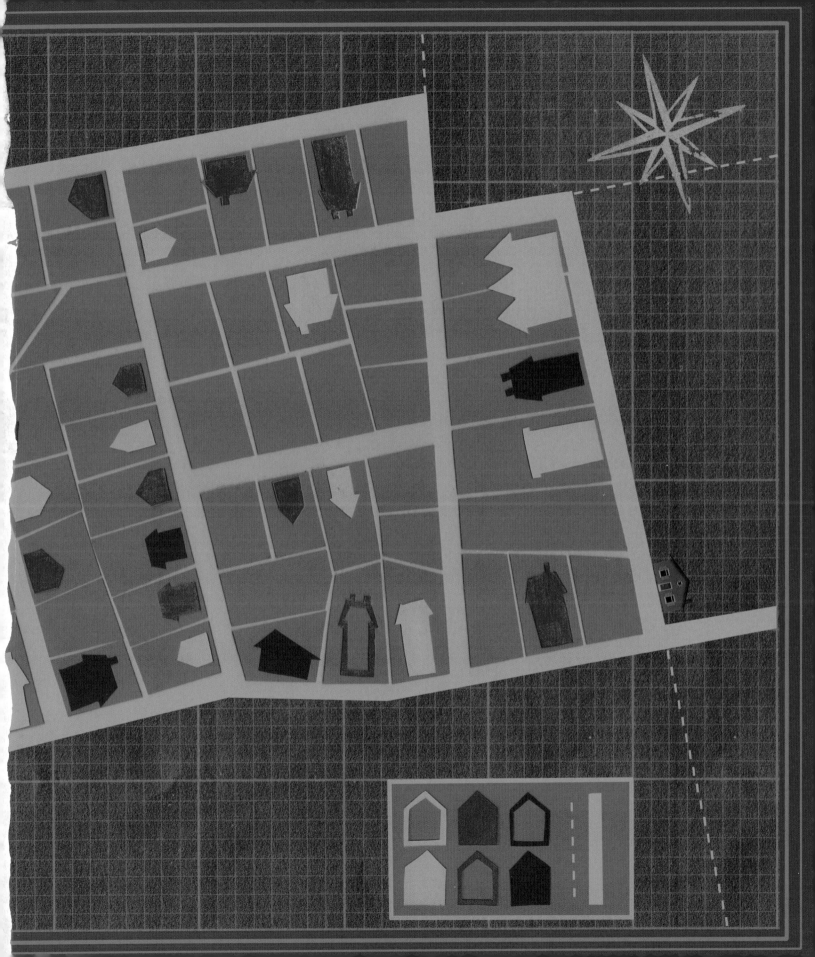

Each time he peeked outside
he saw more of them.

And more.

And more.

And more.

When the last of his field was gone,
he closed his front shutters for good.

Now it was very dark, and very still.

It seemed that even the wind had stopped howling.

Winter came.

But snowdrifts did not push up against him.

Spring showers rained down.

But his shutters did not rattle and slam.

When summer sunshine warmed his rooftop, he cracked open a back shutter for the very first time.

A great big long house stood behind him.

He closed the shutter again.

Very slowly, he opened a side shutter — just a crack.

And there was the house next door.

He saw a curtain waving gently through an open window.

He opened his side shutter a little more and watched the morning sun move across the face of the house next door.

Was he being watched, too?

As the sun rose in the sky he opened the shutter a little more, and then a little more.

A warm breeze blew in.

The neighbor's curtain waved gently, to and fro.

Night fell, and the
window of the house
next door began to glow
with a golden light.

Just like his.

The next morning the little house swung open all his shutters to greet the day.

He saw houses in every direction.

Houses made of wood and bricks, metal and
sticks, concrete and stones.

Houses big and small, beautiful, strange, solid, cobbled, high, low, narrow, wide, elegant and fascinating.

And not one of them knew what
the wind would blow in next.